Life Behind the Pen

Jack Lee

Copyright © 2022 Jack Lee

The moral right of the author has been asserted.

Apart from any fair dealing for the purposes of research or private study, or criticism or review, as permitted under the Copyright, Designs and Patents Act 1988, this publication may only be reproduced, stored or transmitted, in any form or by any means, with the prior permission in writing of the publishers, or in the case of reprographic reproduction in accordance with the terms of licences issued by the Copyright Licensing Agency. Enquiries concerning reproduction outside those terms should be sent to the publishers.

This is a work of fiction. Names, characters, businesses, places, events and incidents are either the products of the author's imagination or used in a fictitious manner. Any resemblance to actual persons, living or dead, or actual events is purely coincidental.

Matador
Unit E2 Airfield Business Park,
Harrison Road, Market Harborough,
Leicestershire. LE16 7UL
Tel: 0116 2792299
Email: books@troubador.co.uk
Web: www.troubador.co.uk/matador
Twitter: @matadorbooks

ISBN 978 1803131 665

British Library Cataloguing in Publication Data.
A catalogue record for this book is available from the British Library.

Printed and bound by CPI Group (UK) Ltd, Croydon, CR0 4YY
Typeset in 11pt Adobe Jenson Pro by Troubador Publishing Ltd, Leicester, UK

Matador is an imprint of Troubador Publishing Ltd

For Grandma, who lived to the ripe age of 89.
Every moment in the 12 years I was with her
will be cherished in my heart.

10.11.2021

3 Limericks

There was once a man from New York,
He accidentally ate a fork.
He stayed up all night,
Tried to sing 'Dark Knight,'
He tried but failed then asked Björk.

There was an old woman named Dee,
She was desperate for a wee.
She is telling me,
She is thirty-three,
She found her pants up a Christmas tree.

There once was a dog called Racy,
His greatest mate was named Daisy.
They went to a dog show,
Later performed judo,
Together they met Alanzee.

Age: 8

Brain Swap – My Hamster

Hello, my name is Lighty!
I am a Russian Hamster.
When it is light, night nighty!
My best friend is Squawker, such a prankster!

However, when it is inky black,
Then, that is when we both run and squeak!
When our house opens, it's time for… a snack!
And then we fill and stock our whole cheeks!

Suddenly, the top of the residence opens,
I know it's the giant and a hand emerges,
It carefully grips me, so I'm not frightened, in!
I play and jump on it's palm (which is extremely large)!

I have a drink, run on the wheel, then it's back to bed!
And I dream of a pet that I could take care of and love.
One with a cute and adorable fearless-looking head!
How I wish I could know and thank the giant above…!

Age: 11

British Wildlife Poem

The amazing animals, that roam the Earth,
All of us are excited with a new-born birth!
We are filled with glee and joy,
Wait… it is a baby boy!

The phenomenal plants and flowers that give us air,
You could grow your own… if you dare!
Then you watch the seedling grow and grow and grow,
Wow, a lovely sight, you want more so again you sow!

The beautiful birds that watch upon us, way up high,
In a flock, they all stupendously in sync, fly!
But some are in great danger of being forever gone,
So, we need to protect them to let them live on.

Now, come the fantastic fish that jump and flow,
In the oceans some are high up, some down low.
Most of our world is filled with water and dancing fish.
Some illegally hunted and eaten greedily on a dish.

Now stand up to save the awesome creatures,
With so many we do not appreciate their first-class features.
From the smallest of ants to the biggest of whales,
If we all do our bit, then we will succeed, not fail.

Lastly, as you choose,
Let them live
Or you will lose
So, if the latter, all will be a myth…

Age: 11

Cinquain poems of all the planets in our solar system

Sun
Hydrogen, helium
Burning, lighting, blazing
The centre of our solar system
Star

Mercury
Smallest, innermost
Boiling, freezing, isolating
Named after the messenger of Roman Gods
Terrestrial

Venus
Hottest, bright
Flaming, flaring, charming
Named after the Goddess of love and beauty
Earthly

Earth
Mankind, wildlife
Raining, chattering, challenging
Our planet's rotation is gradually slowing
Ours

Mars
Reddish, fourth
Bogging, chilling, dying
Named after the God of war
Dry

Jupiter
Largest, oldest
Thundering, lightning, whopping
Named after the King of the Roman Gods
Giant

Saturn
Hydrogen, ringed
Freezing, lagging, gusting
Named after the Roman God of agriculture
Gassy

Uranus
Coldest, watery
Tilting, rolling, amazing
Named after the Greek God Ouranos
Icy

Neptune
Heavy, stormy
Outlying, bewildering, gazing
Named after the Roman God of sea
Blue

Age: 10

Cluckingham Palace

Once there was King Chick,
One day he was sick,
No longer could he click,
Nor kick.

He was married with Queen Cluck,
All the chickens thought she sucked.
She always ate duck,
Because it was thought to be good luck.

Cluck only liked fashion,
It was her all-time passion.
When the eagles raided and took most of the clothes,
 the chickens had to ration.
As she had failed the country her face looked ashen.

Chick however only liked food,
He wasn't in a fashion mood,
All who see him eating food, would think he is very rude!
And that is how he makes everyone's volume subdued!

They had a chick, a prince,
Who liked eating mince,
Ages since.
He says yes to mince but gets mixed up with mints!

Eventually Chick died.
And Cluck sighed,
This was known worldwide.
When Cluck followed Chick's death, they were side by side.

Age: 9

Follow the unseeable

Darkness surrounds me,
The absence of light,
Absence of colour,
Absence of ink on the paper.
Impenetrable darkness fills the scene,
Creation begins,
Dim light starts to appear,
Running out of time.
One line… two… three… and then…four.
I want to get out,
To be free.
The light continues to break the dark,
The light now engulfs the darkness,
Yet I cannot get out,
The light is everywhere.
I cannot follow it,
Then, brighter, as bright as the sun,
Now, it twists and turns,
Morning has come.
I am awake.
The duvet is shoved away.
The bed is made,
The page is printed.
Oh, but it does not stop there.
See, if you follow the light,

You will get nowhere, but if you challenge yourself,
In the darkness, where you cannot see,
The dream will be fulfilled,
The story will be written.
And, you will have achieved what you could not have in the light.

Age: 11

Halloween

This event happens once a year,
People creep up on you from the rear!
Sometimes the joke can be severe,
But mostly mere.

Ghosts, vampires and bats,
There could also be rats,
Or gnats,
Maybe even cats!

Trick or treat they will say,
If it's a treat, they will say YAY!
Other people celebrate Halloween with a buffet!
Halloween is only for a day.

A trick, a curse,
Don't bother seeing the nurse,
The effect is adverse.
There is no reverse!

Halloween happens in the night,
Be careful, they might be on the right,
And then they'll give you a real fright.
You never know, Halloween just might be tonight!

Age: 9

Imagine this…

Imagine a world free of pollution,
Imagine a world rid of barren.
Or a world full of contamination,
And a globe with waste, a million tonnes.

Think of the poor giving to the rich,
Think of the good turning to the bad,
Imagine the rich giving to the poor,
Imagine the bad becoming the good.

Imagine love twisted into hatred.
Dream that happiness meanders to grief.
Imagine loathe revolved to affection.
Dream that melancholy turns to joy.

Imagine the world like a better place,
The universe; one nation and party,
All working together, the human race.
If you dream and *imagine this…*

… it WILL be glee

Age: 11

Jack

Just a good writer.

And a good footballer.

Clever boy.

Keen at reading.

Age: 5

Knocked down

Trapped.
Trapped in our homes,
In our minds,
Our heart, in binds.

Gone.
Gone is the freedom,
The will of life,
Nationwide strife.

Death.
Death is everywhere,
It seems inevitable,
We are mortal, penetrable.

Out.
Out, we can now go,
Restrictions being lifted,
Anxiety being drifted.

Hope.
Hope of a new 'normal,'
Yet it will never be the same,
The losses will not be in vain.

Joy.
Joy will come out of hiding,
It will be released into the atmosphere once more,
The wounds of Earth will be restored.

Life.
Life is a chorus.
Life is gracious.
But most importantly… life is precious.

Age: 12

My Monster

My monster is 15 years old,
She never does what it is told.
Even when I give her what she really wants,
Like croissants!

Her name is Fluffy,
She is very skinny,
But she's a toughie,
She also owns a monkey!

She has very woolly hair,
Which makes fluff float around in the air!
Making it hard not to swallow it,
And my PE teacher always complains why there's
    so much fluff in my PE kit.

The thing that makes her cute is she's only 30cm high,
Which makes her up to my thigh!
Yet she is as loud as an elephant seal,
But she hates eating eels!

She smells like a skunk,
Or you can say a piece of junk!
Whenever I get the whiff of her, I feel all drunk,
Then I dance to the punk!

Her ears are as small as a snail's shell,
She's too cute for me to sell!
So I will wait until she is naughty and then I will get her expelled!
And then she might end up living in a prison cell!

Age: 8

Mothers Day

My mum is the tranquil nightingale's song,
Her voice never goes wrong.
My mum is as pretty as twilight,
So she's obvious in sight!

She drives me to school,
On the weekends, maybe to the pool.
To keep me cool.
When we're back home, there're no rules!

My mum is very caring,
She is the 'helping hand!'
For me, she does everything.
She is the support, she is my righthand.

When I'm not in the best of times,
She amuses me with a handful of mimes!
To me she is prime.
Although when she's drunk, she can do several crimes…!

Age: 10

What shall we do with the grumpy teacher?

What shall we do with the grumpy teacher?
What shall we do with the grumpy teacher?
Early in the morning.

**Hang her from a wooden climbing frame,
Call her a very nasty name.
Don't let her catch you pulling faces,
Put work back in the correct places.
Early in the Morning.**

Ooh ray and up she rises,
Ooh ray and up she rises,
Early in the morning.

What shall we do with the grumpy teacher?
What shall we do with the grumpy teacher,
Early in the morning.

**Put her stinky clothes inside out,
So that she looks like a smelly snout.
Paint her face like an evil witch,
Feed her a wiggly worm sandwich
Early in the Morning.**

Ooh ray and up she rises,
Ooh ray and up she rises,
Early in the morning.

What shall we do with the grumpy teacher?
What shall we do with the grumpy teacher,
Early in the morning.

Rotate her like a never stopping fidget-spinner,
Make a plateful of baked beans for dinner.
She wishes to find her very best mate,
Early in the Morning.

Age: 8

My Friend...

You're my friend no one can replace,
And you're always in my face.
You cheered me along to win a race,
And I got first place.
Now I'm not a disgrace!

When I'm down,
I have a big frown,
But you make yourself a funny clown,
Wearing brown,
And upside down!

Through the following years,
We've been helping each other's fears.
When I need help you're always near,
Especially when I have a tear.
After your support we always have a cheer!

When you come for a sleepover to stay,
We can play all day!
For lunch we'll go to a café,
And for dinner we go for a buffet,
Yay! Hooray!

Age: 8

My Mum

My mum is always beside me,
Never will she be gone,
She's always filled with glee,
And makes sure I do nothing wrong.

She's the warmth in the house,
And I'm never ever alone,
As my dad has a spouse.
And they say I'm worth more than a … phone!

When the devils come,
She hugs me when I am scared.
When their armed with a gun, pointing at the son!
And when we're snared!

My mum is the best thing you can ever dare know,
The most important thing to her she says is … me!
She can always be seen as she's in bright yellow!
She's the best mum you can ever have, now do you see?

Age: 9

My trip to MacDonald Farm

We went to MacDonald Farm,
I tried not to cause any harm.
The farm was 52 acre,
Joe was the lovely caretaker.

We had a 'Scavenger Hunt,'
We also learned about the runt.
We had a trip to the royal Cluckingham Palace!
When the food was out the chickens pecked with malice!

We played many activities,
Their sweet honey was produced from their bees.
The exercises were mainly team building ones!
We were split into two groups, unfortunately, the others won.

Nevertheless, I loved the long zip line,
It was like I was flying!
No… we're going home,
I want to stay. I don't want to get going.

But as soon as I was back
The sleep I lacked,
Was replenished as I slept,
Like a log…

Age: 10

Our teacher likes music

Our teacher likes music,
She sings it all day.
She gets us to work,
So she can go "HOORAY."

She'll sing in her mind,
Singing more and more.
She'll close her eyes,
Suddenly she'll snore.

She daydreams
Singing an opera chorus.
She just never stops, and she is always loud,
It's worse than a circus!

She's worse than me being with an elephant
I can't believe she can't just sit,
UNBELIEVABLE.
Just stop it!

It's finally lunchtime,
We see our teacher.
Guess what she's doing,
She's dancing like a creature.

It is afternoon assembly,
We all dance to the beat.
Our headmaster says
"Please take your seat."

Age: 8

My Creature

My furry creature: dangerous and cruel,
It rummages around looking around for it's gruel.
Searching for it's fuel.
It prances and dances; it jigs and bounds, like a diamond jewel.

Waving it's legs,
Like rickety old pegs,
Round and round and round and raaraaarouuuund liikkkeee
    aaann egggg!
"whooooaaaaa… SSStttoooppp, pppleeease," it begs.

It's going blind,
Already been fined!
Countless times!
For driving with a subconscious mind.

His nose is always blocked,
Waits for me to serve food, waiting like a rock.
Goes to school and gets mocked,
Poor little sock.

His hearing's only getting worse,
We need a nurse.
So it is reversed.
PLEASE, STOP THIS CURSE!

Age: 10

Hamster

Hamster is a clever pet, they never go into a net.

And my Roborovski hamster one, is not even a ton.

Many hamsters can't live long, but sometimes they can even sing a song.

Shh! They are sleeping so don't make them weeping.

Time to play, before they lay.

Every time they eat, they don't want wheat.

Roborovski hamsters are the best, don't make them a real pest.

Age: 7

Once upon a dream...

I was in Mumbles, yes a peculiar name,
But maybe just maybe, it will roar in fame!
'The best holiday place' trophy, they claim,
Mumbles wouldn't be the same.

On the beach, sheathed in sand,
Hearing the music from the band,
The sea as fierce as never before, swept my feet off the land,
Oh, I loved it; how grand!

Next, fresh fried, fabulous fish,
Of course on the dish,
Oh very yummy, my teeth going mish mash mish!
Lemonade on the house, delish!

Oh, the lovely vivid view,
On the leaves, the droplets of dew,
The sky, the sea, mainly blue,
All too good to be true!

Age: 9

Spring

At the beginning of Spring,
My cheek bones tingly ting!

My eyes see the wondrous blue sky,
And the colourfully patterned butterfly.

My ears hear the blow of the breeze,
But the drifting pollen makes me sneeze.

I smell the feast of the cool air,
Including the whiff of the fertilisers, beware!

Morning air whips your tongue,
Your skin is lashed with the combined frost and sun.

Spring makes you feel free,
Like the beaches beauty!

Spring has an elated emotion of joy,
As happy as a baby with an exciting new toy!

When flamingo-like flowers bloom.
In the garden there is lots of room.

The sun shines on the sparkling rivers
While the slimy snake slides and slithers.

The cold, snotty Winter is now in a deep snore,
And now Spring is here, once more.

Spring is a season of glad glee.
Spring is lovely, now do you see?

Age: 10

Superhero Adventure

I was a superhero with superpowers to do this and that. I was on Planet Earth to do only one thing, to save the world from the evil skeleton which is robbing every village, every town, every city…

I used all of my senses to find where the skeleton was.

I used my mouth to lick the floor if I could taste anything suspicious!

I used my nose to check the smell of skeleton bandages.

I used my eye to find footprints or if it was hiding anywhere.

I used my ear to discover the skeleton's location.

Age: 6

Talking Parrot

I wish I had a parrot
I would say, 'Good parrot,'
And say, 'Remember your name, Harry.'
I would teach Harry how to do maths,
Games, English, science and music.
I would also take Harry shopping and on holiday.
As I haven't got a brother or sister,
I just want to be closer to Harry.
Just like a family doing things together.
When I'm in danger Harry will call out his friends to save me.
I'm really hoping Mum and Dad will get me a parrot when I am older.
Mum said that if I look after myself I can look after a pet.

Age: 6

The big poetry party!

Many people rejoice this day,
United, not apart.
Laughing out loud over a tart.
Loudly but lovingly reunited,
Everywhere, the spark is reignited,
Dancing and tumbling wherever you go and…

Wherever you are.
Illuminated by the flashing fairy lights,
Nationwide, this is celebrated.
Everyone, be happy for Christmas is nigh!

Age: 12

Look at the first letter of each line, what word does it spell? …

The Midwinter Night's Dream

It is a cold, chilly, dark monstrous, sinister night,
There is something about it that gives you quite a fright.
It is a long way until there is the break of light.
Through the stormy winds, I drag my feet with all my might!

I come upon a house, maybe there will be a ghost,
If I go in, I'll inevitably become toast!
Or, blood-loving vampires, I really hate them most.
With them, I'll be sure to become a lovely dinner, (roast)!

I know that the house will be packed full of sin,
Nevertheless, I will be brave and go in.
The door shut itself like a magnetic pin.
Ahhhhh! Promptly, I see a man, with gruesome skin!

This cannot be happening, this must be a dream,
It's impenetrable night here, thicker than steam.
And, I need food, although I hate it, I'll even have cream.
Please, I just need a little spark or speck of gleam!

Age: 10

The Notes of Life
(Metaphorical Poem)

(Different notes of instruments
representing different emotions felt in life)

My hands are zooming up and down,
Showing off it's flare.
The chimes of my life,
The twists the turns,
Gifts and the burns.
The genre: the wind,
Percussion, you string,
You're Asian or you're African,
Pop and you rock,
You're British, you're Spanish
You're trombone, piano, you wish!

Try to be Yorkshire, cockney,
Why, you're F sharp, or B flat.
The fingers have a mind
Scaling up, down.
Jumping, flipping
Tumbling, feeling
You live or you lose,
As you choose.
Music is our emotion
Music is different
Music is all around us
Music is our life.

Age: 11

The Tyrant

Once there was a tyrant which was hated, at the least,
Which came from the Middle East.
The toy got covered in yeast,
And with baking hot weather became a beast.

The thing became larger and grew and grew,
Until the whole earth dropped all its dew,
And cows could no longer even go mooooo!
The world shook as everyone ran, when the thing whispered… boo!

The tragic news spread,
Unfortunately a couple already dead,
And survivors fled.
It was worse than the plague with crosses red.

As the dreadful, fading days went by,
Every living person at once made a sigh:
"OH! We're all going to die."
I wish I couldn't see with my eye.

The thing extinguished the last remaining Labrador,
This was only the beginning of the next World War.
Even the children couldn't go to the local candy store!
The devil was given a name… a 'Dinosaur!'

Age: 10

Waiting for Santa

Deck the Halls, the famous song.
On Christmas Day, Big Ben goes ding-dong!

Winter is the season when snow may fall.
Big Ben stands so tall!

Presents are opened on Boxing Day,
HIP HIP HOORAY!

Christmas is your second brilliant birthday,
Everyone should cheer and be happy, not in dismay.

Watch out, Santa Claus may come.
Better lay down some food for his big tum!

Santa Claus, Father Christmas, Saint Nick,
They are the same, and never get sick.

For every good girl and boy
He will give you a toy.

The decorations hang, dangling from the Christmas tree,
Just waiting for Santa to see.

Age: 9

World's best Mum

I love my mum,
She is always number one,
I use to be in her tum,
She's my best chum!

She cooks the best food,
Even when she's not in the best of moods!
And she's never rude!
But she is shrewd!

She helps me in the hard times,
Or when I do crimes,
She pays all of the fines!
And when a question is hard she doesn't tell me the answer, she
    mimes!

She take cares of me,
When I hurt my knee,
Or a sting from a bee!
She's the best mum, now do you see?

Age: 9

Bonfire Night

Bonfire night is a special night,
Everyone crowds around the fire light,
While gasping in amazement to the fireworks sight.
Kids stand back as that is right!

Pets must be away,
Don't keep them stray,
Many will say,
"Keep pets out from the fireworks display!"

Toasting marshmallows and having fun,
Make the most of it before there is sun!
Mums and dads, keep a look out for your son,
As they'll get mixed up with anyone.

Guy Fawkes, a failed man,
Involved in the gunpowder plan,
If it had worked, I do not know what would have happened other than,
Guy Fawkes, a successful man.

Age: 9

The Beginning

I hope you enjoyed reading this book,
Do not fret as more are on its way.
But I've loved your precious face light up.
Eager for some more.

I am sad, maybe you are too,
Well… that depends on your point of view.

As you put this book away for now I must,
Ask for no single speck of dust,
To land on the cover, you, I entrust.
Keep this book secret, guard it with your life, make sure it is
    only read by us.

I know you will not let me down,
Which makes me as happy as a clown.

The joy of our adventures together,
It is not over.
I have loved talking with you,
Through my words.

Thanks for the moments,
They have been brilliant

This book is done,
But the odyssey has just begun,
Now go outside and enjoy the sun (or rain).
I'll see you next time. Have fun!

Age: 12

About the Author

I was born in Surrey, living in Berkshire and currently Wiltshire. I have no siblings but two lovely parents, many friends and 30 hamsters once! I love sports: golf, table tennis, tennis and swimming. Otherwise: chess, piano and… writing (of course!)! Many of my poems were published at 'Young Writers' competitions!